After Words

ALSO BY RAN HUNTSBERRY

POETRY

Movin' On

Drilling Down

Undertow

The Stranger Myself

NONFICTION

Listening Out Loud: The Leadership Paradox

*Creative Listening: Overcoming Fear in Life &
Work*
with Cheryl Varian Cutler

FORTHCOMING

Still Listening

After Words

Ran Huntsberry

Book Layout by Karen Douglass

Back Cover Text first appeared in SPILLWAY,
No. 9, Spring/Summer, 1999

ACKNOWLEDGEMENTS

With gratitude to my friends and family who always have my back, especially my Gamut colleagues and friends, Julie Ascarrunz, Ruth Bull (deceased), Frank Coons, Jane Costain, Karen Douglass, Lew Forester, Sheryl Luna, Vicki Mandell-King, Elizabeth Oxley, Carmella Santorelli, Judy Satterlee, and Penelope Barnes Thompson, all of whom have shared their own poems and critiqued mine on a weekly basis for nineteen years. They, along with Liz Rees, are my "co-authors."

Special thanks to Karen Douglass for her willingness to put together yet another collection for Gamut Press, my grandson, Kaden Hawley, for generating the front cover, and Vicki Mandell-King for always giving me an extra mile.

Though for some years now, I have not been submitting individual poems for publication, the following poems have appeared in various iterations in the following publications:

Journal of Ethnic Studies - "Mud Creek"
Muse of Fire - "Morning After"
Phoenix - "I Swear to God"
Poetic License - "Hang Up"
Rainbow Review - "After Words"
Thorny Locust - "Grave Digger Tales"

To my dear friends and family,

for your courage and never failing humor.

Thank You!

CONTENTS

I

II

AFTER WORDS

You complain my words
might seem more friendly
a little less intentionally oblique,
that I'm just too two-sided
to come down clean
and say what I mean.

True enough, but for me
making harbor
requires much tacking.
I never arrive anywhere
straight-on.

And besides,
when you tell it back,
I've always said more
than I meant,
and all I can do is smile
and race to catch up
to wherever my words
have blown you.

I

The Truth must dazzle gradually
Or every man be blind.
~ Emily Dickinson

MY WORDS

dangle
in between

untangle
breath from meaning

blow
my freaking mind

kick
my stupid ass

UNCLE REMUS TALES
~as told by Gramma Huntsberry

I still remember cold mornings
hunkered down beside your pot-bellied stove
and you telling these far-fetched
Brer Rabbit stories in the heaviest drawl
I'd ever heard about how Brer Fox
tricked Brer Rabbit into punching
his Tar Baby *contrapshun* cuz Tar Baby
didn't offer a *spectubble Good Mawnin*
and so Brer Rabbit got all stuck up
till he couldn't get away without tricking
Brer Fox into throwing him
into his favorite briar patch
where he knew Brer Fox couldn't follow
and then laughing his way out the other side.

Of course, you never revealed
these stories came from slave narratives.
I just knew playgrounds were dangerous,
and trickery was the smart way
to stay on top in the pecking order
like the time I tricked Mr. Hoover
into believing it was Leon Huff's fault
we were fighting cuz I was only trying
to protect the helpless girls, and so
Leon got a severe paddling
that left him a tear-stained, butt-stung mess,
while I pranced down the hall
laughing my fool head off.

DIVINE COMEDIES

You say we need something
to save us from ourselves, an enemy
to run against, even if
it means a few bruises.

I ask are names carved
on stone tablets
any better than fly-paper
in a church window?

You say it takes guts
to sculpt a god worth the killing
so we can't back down now,
even if they stone us.

I ask what about the Buddha
if you meet him on the road
or Jesus on the cross?

You say worst case,
if you fall for your own creation,
make him die laughing.

THE PASTOR'S PARROT

Open up your funky mind and you can fly.
~ George Clinton, *Funkadelic*

In the pastor's house,
there's a lot of preaching going on.
Even his parrot shrieks
bright orange and green
when I invade his sacristy,
like he's been bushwhacked
by the devil himself.

Doesn't he know
I'm on his side
preaching of times before
cages and clipped wings?

Has he forgotten
what it was like before the Fall,
when he flew in the Garden,
even soared a little?

Is it so blasphemous,
my scant faith
in morning crumbs
and the pastor's firm hand
bearing us cage to cage?

PROUD SINNER

Curiosity is the beginning of all sin.
~ Bernard of Clairvaux

Great-Grandma Ham
was always laughing at me
for what she called
my *boarding house reach,*

when as far as I knew
I was just another runt
with no reach at all,

and when she scolded
Curiosity will surely be
the death of that boy
I sensed she was secretly
applauding the sinner in me,

like she knew all along
I only wanted
to shinny up her apple tree
for that one last prize
just out of reach.

CENTER STAGE

~ San Francisco, February, 1980

a Woody Guthrie sound-alike
sings to a Cannery crowd
of exuberant hippies
while across town Julie Harris
plays Emily Dickinson
with more prudence
than a Puritan
and next door in an open park
a ballerina partners with a chair
falling   out of it   over it
like slapstick Charlie

or like me some years before
when three esteemed professors
and I were lecturing
on the futility of religious practice
in a secular world
and found ourselves unbelievably
confronted by a wacky front row crush
of screaming groupies
who knocked my straight-backed conceit
upside down pushing and shoving
so desperate for attention
that I fled the hall vowing never
to mount another stage
so help me god

OUTED
> ~ to R. Johnson, Editor, 1979

Flattened down dumb! After twenty years,
I finally tell somebody and all you can say
is *What modern poets are you reading?* I feign

Who have you got in mind? (Oh god, how stupid!)
Simic, Merwin or . . . (the last I miss). I stutter
Ashbery, I don't much like and I'm still reading Frost
(silence)*'cause I used to hear him at Sanders Theatre*
when he was old and I was young writing mushy love
poems back to Montana, and 'cause he loved
freshness, trout in particular,
I brought him some one Christmas break
hot-iced 2000 miles by train (silence)

and oh did I mention lunch with Simic last January,
and how I used to sneak into MacLeish's lectures
on Dickinson and Eliot 'cause I was too nervous
to sign up, though I did wonder
how Eliot would have fared if Pound
hadn't taken him so seriously (more silence).

Bottom line, I have to confess,
mostly I read the women
for their mystifying slant on things.

WHAT'S TO DIE FOR?

Poetry is respected only in this country. There's no place where more peopleare killed for it.

~

Osip Mandelstam

no matter what you say
no one around these parts
will care enough to shoot you
or hang you or cut your tongue out
or even mutilate your fancy book cover
unless some critic takes notice
and attacks your poem for malaprops
and lazy turns of phrase even claiming
your whole corpus D.O.A.
'cause no one gets locked up
for calling the president a fascist pig
and no one water-boards a poet
to shut him up let alone
make him talk 'cause these days
even the great poets
are only good for inaugurals
and celebrations of war
something beyond any personal cost
but the oblivion of dust

THE SEUSSIAN CHALLENGE
~ for Claire at 7 years

teacher says
a *blank* in a *blank*
allows room for *something*
in *something* else
but when she demands
cat in the first blank
and leaves you to choose
between *basket* or *lap* in the second
you raise your hand
and tell her
Go read the book
for after your *cat* in a *cap*
wins no smiley face
and you've given up
on *bubble gum* and *underwear*
you insist over dinner
That teacher's a pain in my brain
only Suess can reduce
and *that* is the end of *that*

A NOTE FROM THE DEAF-MUTE LANDLADY

You bang on the ceiling
with a broom handle,
send your son upstairs with a note
to calm our linoleum beat
and your dancing chandelier.

Right to hammer or saw somethings
if you need to make anytimes but not late
in the night. Right to play the ping pong
if you need but don't get active
to move the furnitures or jump and ran
to get a ball. Joe and I can feel the pressures.
Do you know about the children ran or jumping
make the ceilings cracked?

Timid, the boy voices what you feel,
and from then on, we tiptoe barefoot
over your noisy world.

RESONANCE AT THE EMPIRE TAVERN

Thursday night and the lounge
is not too noisy. I can almost
hear the music.

After the first set,
I meet a *fellow poet*
who informs me
Thirty-four years ago I got
brain damage in the First Gulf War,
and I've been on disability ever since.
I write poems so my brain will feel
the resonance embedded in the words.

Resonance heals, he insists,
his words cobbled together,
one halting syllable at a time.

NEXT TO LAST STOP
~ on the MTA, Boston

Daydreaming about what's next, I notice a disheveled
man standing beside me on the platform staring at his
shoes. He looks up, does a quick survey, says *Good
morning,* then exclaims *Look at that*! and jumps four
feet down onto the tracks. I try not to think about
the third rail.

He comes up staring at my shoes. Sensing my need,
he says *Somebody threw a penny down here,
can you believe it? Good money too!* He stoops over.
One, he calls out, then *Two*.

He hops back on the platform and extends his hand.
*My name is Stephen. Whoa! There's another one!
Look, it's almost black.* Thankfully, still no train.

After that, I just listen. He says, *Right now, I get by
on my disability check, but I make a lot of beer money
collecting etched-out lottery tickets
from grocery store dumpsters. Can you believe it?
Once I found one worth a hundred bucks.*

Suddenly, he stops mid-sentence and vaults back
onto the tracks. *It's a gold mine down here.*
We laugh together loud and hard. *Won't be long
till I'm ridin for nothun. How about you?*

I SWEAR TO GOD
~ at a psychiatric hospital, 1976

Every day residents roam the halls hoping
to catch a glimpse of *Crazy Christa* retching
towards heaven, her chalk-white teeth chomping
on a hand full of *papal* pastry.

Into the night we hear her pounding
her *fuck-you-mans* out on a huge organ.
Her dirge sets bones dancing in the choir.

In the morning she confesses
to a friendly Jesuit stroking her cheek
God gets down on me every night
and twice on the full moon
just because I'm Jewish,

but her confessor maintains
his immaculate misconception
that *No one fucks with God,*
which sets her off chanting
Go fuck yourself, Go fuck yourself

as she struts down the hall,
her plastic cross hoisted high
and upside down, giving voyeurs
at every turn a divine middle finger.

IN AND UNDER

The school board can't understand
        why all the fuss
about *Under God* being pledged
        in every school.

McCarthyites don't care
        if *In God We Trust*
causes a substantial burden
        for a bunch of godless Commies.

After all, it's for the children's sake
        E Pluribus Unum
even while cynics question
        Under Whose God?

Hoarders complain
        I need One,
while tax paying citizens maintain
        In God We Trust is our civic duty.

Blacks (and a few Whites)
        sing *Hallelujah*, and just today,
with a simple handshake,
        a young protester
forgave an old white man in cowboy boots
        for kicking him in the balls.
If only he was listening.

I I

*Where can I find a man
who has forgotten words?
I would like to have a word with him.*
~ Chuang Tzu

YOUR WORDS

steam out of hot showers
like random wild flowers
strewn on a hillside full of weeds

echo out of caves
too dank
to read by

blow out of love letters
embedded
in endless sand

twist out of whack
neck-deep
in laughter

SUNDAY MORNING PUZZLES

Who would suffer cross
words to make sense
of questions
hidden in the attic?

Yet Sunday mornings,
driveway anomalies arrive
in green plastic bags,
and during breakfast

I search for answers
left to right,
while meaning escapes
on the vertical.

PROPER ETIQUETTE

A friend tells me
how he Googles up answers
during dinner conversations
with the same diligence
he applies to his daily crosswords,
but he admits his compulsion
to cross-check
his new bride's every thought
does interrupt
the flow between them.

One day, after much wrangling,
he abandons his iPhone
for his beloved Glock
and casually begins to polish the barrel
clamped between his legs.

Lucky for him, when the gun goes off,
he only shoots himself in the foot,
but from that day forward
his between-screams bride
demands iPhones only.

RIGHT WORDS

caught too often
with my foot in my mouth

I used to think the right word
if I could only find it

would extract me
from even the deepest ditch

but most often like today
I'm horrified by what shows up

a single word protesting
at the top of its lungs

then collapsing
into irrelevance

even as I scan
for another *right* word

my mouth puckered tight
like a contrite kiss

OLD THINKING
~ after Robert Hass

Endings
incubate unseen
sure as clockwork.

Parentheses
bend back upon themselves.
Some show up, some don't.

Hypotheses
rest on vagaries of sun and rain,
how rich the soil, how pregnable.

Antitheses
sleep with their opposites,
full of questions.

SO IT APPEARS

from the beginning
I never really knew
who my mother was
or for that matter
any of the women
who came after her

'cause all these years
I never knew what I didn't know
or the questions I needed to ask

and even if I had
none of the women
would have known
what was at stake

at least till the day
I felt secure enough
to risk groping
into the mystery
of who they really were

TOO SOON

Beneath mulchy mid-winter leaves,
the gardener discovers a thorny shoot
low off the trunk. Before summer's end,
will it honor its promise?

~

Early spring, the blood rose
stands frozen, three buds
too soon committed.

~

Reflection makes floating
difficult – curiosity weighs lake-heavy.
Half-way under, blue sky turns green.
Thoughts surface with a different cast.

~

Sunset, five planets line up
head-over-heels, the moon
weaving between them
like a lost lover.

~

Years ago, a beautiful woman
stood framed in a doorway.
Afterwards, nothing held.

RUG-BURN

the morning sun glares
through the window
at your naked spine

and the ripe strawberry
you bear
from a lover's dare
laid on the carpet

a first ember
of the wildfire
yet to come

5 A.M. FARM REPORT

we wake just as blue
is breaking on the skylight
above our Queen Anne bed
the gray mist glistening
like dissolving faces
as our bodies contract
under mounds of covers
like shriveled mummies
hoping for enough heat
to generate something

MORNING AFTER

      she rises —
legs
      oblique twigs —
eyes
      faded cumulus —
body
      empty sack —
breasts
      wasted moon cheese —
fingers
      nervous swamp grass —
desire
      taut catgut —
heart
      buttered squash —
skin
      shriveled mummy —
words
      untuned keyboard —
hope
      flat as a punctured tire —

LEAVINGS

Corralled, she rides her horse
in methodical circles

while he sits in the window,
a black cat curled in his lap.

One day, she whispers
I'm leaving,

and the cat yowls
and dashes into the forest.

Neighbors report sightings
miles around. Nothing

checks out. Eventually,
he gives up.

Neither returns.

LAST PUT DOWN

when it comes time to part
she divides the family
photos in doggie bags
but keeps the dog for herself
not me in my prime
even though if it's freedom she wants
I can still walk myself even
drive my own car but of course
she can't stick me
in a kennel when she wants
a weekend off though
that never stopped her
so okay I have to admit
I feel a little insulted
being put down
before the dog
and even worse
she says she's adding
another after the move
and I laugh to myself too bad
I never learned any new tricks

AND YET

Our secrets required lies
till the two reversed
and we mistook one
for the other and yet
I still regret
what we left behind.

Words did shield us
from the mirror of ourselves
and yet how foolish we were
panning Eden's stream
like gold rush miners
grubstaking the promise
and yet never panning
a single nugget.

CONCEALED WEAPONS
~ after The Tale of Genji

A smile –
    after church

A handshake –
    behind an embrace

Designer labels –
    inside the collar

Desire –
    in a studded box

A Trojan horse –
    outside the gate

A lover –
    hanging by a semblance

A love poem –
    morning after

BIDING TIME

This morning you pose
a casual question — *What can I do
with you? I'm married.*

I imagine a side drawer,
a place on your husband's bookshelf,
or maybe the weeping willow drooping
over your back fence. But no . . . .

Late afternoon
on the hill behind your house,
blinding snow clings
to our eyelashes
as neighbor children
butt-slide down shrieking.

NOT QUITE

Montana
stretches beyond
a dream I once had
too broad
to get my arms around

a dream of swimming
your mighty Yellowstone
and being sucked
into endless whirlpools

a dream of scouting
your grasslands
for a break
in the horizon

a dream of painting
your body naked
along the Rim Rocks
before sunset

a dream of seeds
germinating in your fields
harvesting more
than your Big Sky

CONDITIONS OVERRIDE

The sky is deadly dark
when her husband returns
from an extended business trip

yet he allows her
to take her lover
for one last walk
around the block admonishing

If you don't come back
I'll take the children and God
will get your soul. And, remember,
since passion fizzles
in a fortnight,
you'd just as well
give it up now

and by the time they return,
she has.

A DIFFICULT TRANSLATION

So what does it mean –
our knees touching

under the table,
your fingers

laying words
gently on the back
of my hand?

Was it desire or
simply a casual habit?

And why did your touch
deepen into tears?

CURSES

morning-after
      a single strand
on my pillow
      the color of
Malibu sand
      marking
your territory
      with a curse
so delicate
      an interloper
would flee
      and never know
why

TELL ME MORE
~ after Emily Dickinson

stuck in no man's land
with a need for discretion
the downward glance

he sips the silence
until at last
she speaks her mind

and that changes
everything

A CERTAIN DAY
~ for Joan & Andy, July 29, 2007

as if each day isn't
special enough
with its slight bends
and quotidian gestures

a certain day warranting elevation
more than any other

a day beyond imagination
revealing a certain rhythm
more remarkable than anything
that's gone before

a day certain to change
the way you see
the past surpassed
and anticipate the future

a fanfare of comets streaming
beyond this particular day
making certain the universe
is forever altered

III

Tell all the Truth but tell it slant.
~ Emily Dickinson

NOT TO PANIC

day after day I pull my red wagon
around the block looking for somebody
besides the girl next door
who makes me play wounded soldier
to her tender nurse unlike
the Gunther boys down the road
where I'll never venture again
after they accuse me
of being a Nazi traitor
for breathing too much air
and that I'm gonna die
unless I hold my breath
the whole way home
which I do
at least long enough
to make it terrified back to Mother
laughing at a radio preacher
trying to convince Borneo tribesmen
they'll all go to hell
for their faith in tall trees
even as she assures me
there's air enough
and it isn't the end of the world
like the time she swore
all the way home that the sudden wind
blasting us in the face would not destroy
my new kite whipping hard
against my backside till finally
standing in our Victory Garden
I gave it string enough
to breathe sky

DUG IN

Let's find something still alive
Left to kill.
                    ~ Cynthia Cruz

not long after VE-Day
we stand around in the blazing sun
watching columns of red ants come and go
in Grandma's front yard trying to figure out
how these robotic creatures maintain
such militant discipline even after
we cherry bomb their sandy mound
blowing grit to kingdom come
bodies flying every which way
flooding the survivors with buckets
of boiling water and flaming gasoline
and still they keep coming
infiltrating Steve's diaper
for a tender butt-feast
till Mom shows up and sees
his monkey-red ass
and calmly questions
Isn't there something better
you boys could be doing
so we give it up and camp out
in the ultimate safety
of Grandma's porch swing
flying high over Nazi panzers
and the certain glory
of victories yet to come

THE GREAT TERMITE WAR

One morning Dad says *I heard 'um singin'*
under there. Wooden fruit drives termites crazy,
and if we don't stop 'um, they're gonna eat
Gramma's foundation clean out from under her.

Besides the throbbing sound,
and Gramma's more-than-usual
sagging floors, we can't be sure,
so Dad has me squeeze under
the house smelly as a frontline trench
to check it out.

It's pitch black, and I can't feel much
sawdust 'cause termites eat inside out.
But, when I stick my ice pick
into the beams, they're soft as cotton candy.

That's all the evidence we need.
Rotten to the core, but hoping
to keep Grandma from turning
into bone dust under her own floor,
I smear joists with black gunk so thick
they smell like railroad ties.

Since then, I've kept my pick ready,
listening to the dark sounds
underneath.

POOL CLOSED
~ Tulsa, 1950

People say we can't go
swimming anymore cuz we'll get polio
and our lungs will freeze up
like those iron lung kids
in *Life* magazine laid out
flat on their backs
in oxygen tents, like the time
Hodges rolled me up
in the bedroom rug
and I nearly suffocated.

Kids who survive
wear steel braces on their legs,
but they don't come out anymore.

Half a block down,
the Willis boys die,
but nobody talks about it.
We just head for the fields,
strip down and jump head-on
into farmer Mac's scummy cow pond
brimming with leeches.

KILLING DAYS
~ on Oswego Street

evenings we jail pinheads of light in fruit-jars
their bodies throbbing for release

while other nights we throw rocks skyward
for bats to dive bomb

stake out butterflies like brilliant crucifixes
skin dead rabbits and nail them to the garage wall

lie for hours under thick hedgerows
BB gunning sparrows for the body-count

the same old crow always teasing us
just out of range

till one day we hit him
and he flies off screeching

at our impotent gall

MUD CREEK

Sweat pours down every crack — down crusted red clay
— down Arkansas quicksand — down — down

Spit-cotton dry — mud scow dreams
floating to the Gulf of Mexico

Chase cottontail into drain pipe —
boy crawls in head-first — stuck in the mud

Garden gone — shoe-box baby dies — out of season

Weeping tree — switch-cut whipping —
makes the man

On the St. Louis overnight — boy smashes
coke bottles on passing poles — dreams ricochet

Mud Creek — footprints harden — dreams crack

Outhouse condemned — old woman swears any dog
knows shitting inside is unnatural

Hang-head days — boy roars '39 Buick back and forth
across the front yard — faking licensed way out

Mud Creek — dry as squirrel bone — off bridge
gunny sack full of kittens — none escape — not one

WHERE DO WE GET OFF?
~ for Rosa Parks, December 1, 1955

She took a back seat
to no one. *Uppity!*
people said.

Maybe she just figured
her behind deserved
nothing less
than any other.

Of course, the passengers
went crazy and the driver
shouted *Lady, I told you.*
Get to the back of the bus.

But she just planted
herself rigid as a flag pole
and refused to budge,
leaving me wondering
When do I get on?

TRAILS OF TEARS

During the hard winter of 1838-39, President Andrew
Jackson ordered 15,000 Cherokees removed, Georgia
to Oklahoma. Along the way, 4000 died.

...the defect of the system was apparent. ... There is
no selfishness, which is the bottom of civilization.
~ U.S. Senator Henry Dawes, after visiting
The Five Civilized Tribes in Oklahoma, 1887

Rumor had it Grandpa was half Cherokee, but
more likely, he was half of nothing before a white
preacher adopted him, though it didn't make much
difference cuz he never owned any property,
odd-jobbing all his life.

As a teenager, Dad was so poor he propositioned
the owner of the old caboose diner where he worked
before and after school, claiming that since nobody
had any money, especially including him, he'd buy
the diner with cash from the daily till. Before long,
the whole family was frying five cent burgers
and watching out for Gypsies with hundred dollar bills
they couldn't break.

Later on we followed Dad, oil field to oil field.
Friends left behind were counted good as dead,
cuz once we set out, we had no homeland, just trails
crying in all directions.

IN MY FATHER'S EYE
~ for MDH

How many times I ran away
barely out of diapers. What
was I hunting for? I think you knew.

To this day, I ponder your escape
from the blazing fields of Oklahoma,
where you picked cotton
till your hands bled,
a child too small
to drag a bag half full
along the gritty rows.

Like you, when I left for Vienna
and then Japan, I never looked back,
even when Steve left for Vietnam
and Mom had *No son to talk to.*

You used to impute my contrary ways
to my East Coast college days,
and on hindsight, you had a point –
each border crossed
enlarged my appetite.

Come to think of it,
you gave me everything
you ever wanted,
especially my ticket out.

LOST FOR GOOD

all I remember
is forever leaving
though I can't really say
how one place
differed from any other
or whether there was anything
in the last place
that would generate
a story worth telling
or set me apart
from hungry tourists hunting
the perfect souvenir
yet missing the fabric
binding people together
since real tourists stay glued
to roads well-marked
for fear of getting lost
while I've found getting lost
is the best way to find
what I'm not looking for
if only I can keep from
running out of gas
or getting mugged
or worse yet
ending up where I never
wanted to be anyway
all safe and secure

WORD HAD IT

I thought I was something special ...
well maybe ... but what?
Mother always assumed the best,
that I'd protect little Steve
from playground bullies,
and that I was not as bad
as Billy B. who got written up
in the paper for stealing a '49 Ford
on his morning paper route.

Dad feared I'd flunk out of school
and never get into college,
even though college nearly killed him,
flipping depression-era burgers
every waking hour he wasn't in class.

Word had it that my classmates
never knew what to make of me.
I felt safe, leaving them guessing,
never able to pin me down
to something they could get
their heads around.
And what would that be anyway?

THE OTHER SIDE
~ for Roz, 1964

By the time we docked in Yokohama,
the weather had turned on us. Within hours
we discovered our new house had no heat,
and our bath no hot water. Feeling out of control,
we dug up a few weeds out back,
and turned the useless tub
into an indoor *flower* bed.

Desperate, every afternoon we walked
to the public bath standing pristine
next door to the bath owner's battered junkyard.
We were almost always first in line, but
one afternoon, we found ourselves behind
a wartime amputee whose body — what was left of it —
was tattooed head to foot with gaudy demons.

Stark naked, the old man took my finger,
and giggling like a machine gun at my awkwardness,
coaxed me to push against the tattoo on his chest.
To my horror, the demon stayed depressed
with a slight quiver of life all its own,
like I'd penetrated the flesh of War.

RUSH HOUR IN TOKYO
~ 1965

as *Pushers* pack commuters into trains
heavy with humidity and the thick smell
of soy sauce a young schoolgirl
her face smothered in the crush
leans her head back
on her book bag gasping for air
her shoulder crowd-driven
into my ribs while downtown
young men with razor blades
amuse themselves slicing
the calves of women stepping
onto crowded commuter busses
their kimonos stretched so tight
they feel nothing
before the pool of blood

SURVIVAL

~ for Fiona at 5 years

Five hatchlings in a congested nest,
mother bobbing in the grass
listening for worms.

One day, the chicks launch
a most daring landing at our feet,
mother squawking.

Then, for three successive mornings,
we find yet another chick dead.
You puzzle *Why?* I whisper
Don't know.

We shift our attention to the two survivors,
how they scurry to their mother whenever
she freezes, head cocked — sure sign of a worm.
You nod. You get it.

IV

Is there more? More than love
And death? Then tell me its name.
                    ~ Emily Dickinson

LOCKED-IN
~ for Maureen

even now I get anxious
thinking about your grandfather locked
in his body-abandoned brain twitching
to questions posed by researchers scurrying about
with electrodes inside out trying to separate speech
from muscle and give thought the power of direct
action in a silence too near being buried alive

and too near his battered trunk locked
full of forgotten memorabilia you discovered last
weekend helping your parents move off their farm
a trunk full of your great aunt's magic cures
underneath some letters exchanged during the War
along with two and a half pairs of button shoes

and your grandfather's tablet scribbled
after radiation fried his throat
with pages full of words
he never said out loud
words offered up a generation before
his out-and-out lock-in
recounting his panic in jungle foxholes
a panic still twitching
in the mirror each morning
when he tries to shave

LOCKED-OUT
~ for Shannon

your divorce is mine all over again
but since I live with you
and the children
and we have to downsize
I face the necessity
once again of getting rid
of half my library
where every page is underlined
highlighting my lifelong fear
of moving ever closer
to a mind locked
out of touch
with too little room
for the familiar
and too little time
for the unknown

LEFT BEHIND
~ for Roz

I still feel a sense of grief
maybe even guilt
over those Sunday mornings
driving downtown
some sixty years ago
to fetch your Irish grandfather
sitting stiff in the overstuffed lobby
of the Northern Hotel full
of wobbly old men
in high-backed chairs
dressed to the nines
like mourners at a wake
waiting as they did every Sunday
for something to happen
hoping to the man
we might take one of them with us
before we left them behind
for good

LEARNING TO FORGET

when I was a first grader struggling
to stay upright on my first bike
Mom kept coaxing me
to stick with it promising
Once you've done it
your body will never forget
though she never did explain
why Great-Grandma Ham's
one hundred year old body
forgot how to walk
and a couple of falls later
finally it killed her
leaving me confused even now
since Mom danced
till the day she died
but couldn't remember
my name

LETTER TO MARGARET ATWOOD
~ reading at The Intersection,
San Francisco, February, 1980

your words fade in and out
over the smoke-thick crowd
desperately envious
of your international acclaim
and your quirky wild hair
which not one of us can begin
to match and all we can do
is feast on your every twist and turn
your sharp nose and hypnotic eyes
your monotone smile
everyone laboring
to worm inside
your voice so dry
so impossible to capture

LEFTOVERS

Everyone assumed
she'd be forever beautiful
until she wasn't.
He too stood out —
an obvious match.

Then one day, old age took both
her beauty and his memory.
Slow dancing and fine food
no longer satisfied.
Nothing did.

He proposed delicious
alternatives, but always ended up
listening to her celebrate
how good her life had been.
He was good at that.

DEAD SILENCE
~ for Gramma Whiles, d. 1958

Embedded in your casket
as if for your regular
after-lunch catnap,
I feel lonely for you
as I always have. Seems
you were entombed like this
our whole time together.

Something was always missing.
Your spine never bent, even when
I set your garage on fire. I wonder,
was it your nervous breakdown
after your too-young husband
died singing in the church choir?

At your funeral, we find out
our mother was adopted.
Rumor has it she was a half-breed
someone handed to you on the bridge
out of Choctaw Territory.

No matter, you've always lived
in another world. Tell me,
what is it like over there?

NO TRESPASSING

You dared us that winter
to sneak into the quarry
on the next full moon
and dive butt-naked
thirty feet down
into a black pool
full of submerged cars.

We laughed like orangutans
at your desire for cold water
and a broken neck anything
to shatter the mirror
of your empty life

till one night
I found myself standing
on the lower bank
watching your silhouette against
the moonlight marble black
listening to your echo slide
down the sandstone cliff
like Narcissus screaming
at his own face.

DEAD HEAT

sometimes I feel
like a runner
in an ultra-marathon
craning to discern
what will falter first

     mind or body

even though
I know full well
the course is uneven
and no matter which gains
the momentary edge

     dropped words
     or acquired pain

both will cross the finish-line
in a dead heat

GRAVE DIGGER TALES

contrary to common sense

the grave digger boasts of

mid-winter graves

when surface

moisture finally

touches sub-moisture

but his wife demurs

Don't believe a god damn

word he says

but then adds

with a slight grin

It's kinda romantic though

this meeting of

two worlds

like when

pious believers

certified Padre Pio's

miracle of

open wounds

closing

after fifty years

without a scar

as he lay dying with

stigmata

so terrible

even doubting

Thomas probed

with rubber gloves

FIELDS OF BATTLE

What passing-bells for those who die as cattle?
~ Wilfred Owen

Death comes
in its own good time
impatient at the impudence
of wailing families, surgical heroics,
dreams of distant fields.

Death reverses
present conditions
and turns them upside-down,
burning promises to ash.

Death sticks
to its own seductive chores,
knowing only it survives
in dreamless graves.

OUTCOMES

As a child, I used to wonder
when old Fella died
would he end up
in doggy heaven
like the neighbor kids promised,
or would he get reborn
a cat as punishment
for the way he harassed
poor Ebony all those years?

Or would he end up
in a trash can forgotten
in the excitement
of a new stray?

Or would he end up
a memory of the time
he disappeared
for several days chasing
some bitch in heat
before he turned up,
filthy and torn,
bouncing with excitement
just to be home?

NOTHING IN COMMON
~ 60th high school reunion,
Billings, Montana, 2017

I don't remember the face, let alone your name.
I suspect we were strangers, even then. With nothing
to reminisce about, you mention you're retired
and spend most of your Montana time outdoors
enjoying the elk and bighorn sheep.

Latching onto this thin thread, I exclaim *I bet*
you're a birder too. You smile *Yes, of course.*
It's amazing how much we didn't see
before we retired.

I agree, and launch into the topic
of my morning dog walks
and how in one particular spot,
there's always a bunch of stink bugs
scurrying about doing their business.
I confess *When I was younger,*
I would have crushed them
just for the hell of it. Now,
I tiptoe among them.

With this, you begin to back away.
Afterwards, I wonder if I offended you,
ranking stink bugs up there
with your big horn sheep,
as if they too deserved to live.

HANGING MID-AIR
~ for Vicky and Jeremy

It takes us all week
to find the hummingbirds, the ones
we saw in Eldorado Canyon
a few years back when Jeremy could still
get around. I feel like I've let you down
when I can't find them
our first day out.

Then on our last evening together,
we drive further up the canyon
and there they are hovering
at the end of a dirt road,
wings-a-blur over a red feeder,
while we stand gravity bound
a few feet away.

After I drop you at the airport,
I buy the exact same feeder
and hang it outside our kitchen window.
A week later, Jeremy faces another surgery,
while out back, still no hummingbirds.

LEGACIES
~ for Jeremy

two days after your last surgery
we joke long distance
about your continuing *diaper troubles*
and how worried you are
about visitors getting caught up
in your mess and how you faced
the same problem a month ago
as guest of honor at a ritzy
New York banquet celebrating
the new university chair
endowed in your name
and what it was like
sitting center stage
listening to wealthy alumni
applaud your many gifts
over the last fifty years
even as you were smiling to yourself
at what a legacy it would be
if standing in this overwhelming glare
you shat your pants

A LAST GIFT
~ for Penina & Myron Glazer

After fourteen years of steady decline,
you collapse during your annual visit to Florida.
After a painful trip back to Massachusetts,
Penina and the kids decide you've suffered
long enough and it's time to let you go.
For my part, I want to hear how
your gentle humor has held up,
but it feels too intrusive to ask.

A couple of days later, I confess to Penina
how, in an odd dream the night before,
you had demonstrated your humor
was doing just fine. In the dream,
you had already died, but for some reason
had come back and were rummaging
through your old hospice room.
When I asked what you were doing,
you said you were just cleaning up
for the next guest.

By now Penina is chuckling
as she confirms my dream really nailed you,
and I think to myself *Thanks, old friend,*
for this one last laugh.

HIGH DESERT FLOOD
~for my brother, Jon Stephen & his wife, Kathy

The E.R. is packed with broken bodies forced together in this desolate place, maybe cuz they favor the isolation of rural Arizona, and it's sand cheap. All afternoon, staff call out patient names, and after some three hours we hear *JOHN,* but before you can stand up, a burly motorcycle dude from across the room shouts *YAH.* Five minutes later, we hear another *JOHN,* but again, it's not you. By this time, we're beginning to chuckle at this room full of JOHNS, even as we quietly affirm none of them would want to steal your place in line, you with a hole in your belly for food, a hole in your neck for air, unable to talk, with your lower teeth scheduled to be pulled and after that chemo and radiation to destroy the tumor in your throat born of Agent Orange in Vietnam. And besides, your JON is missing a letter. A few minutes later, we hear another *JOHN,* and a disheveled lady with a big tobacco voice shouts *WRONG JOHN* just as a one-legged sailor raises his fist. We stifle our guffaws best we can. Finally they call *JON,* and eventually determine you need another trache. Kathy and I head home, but not a half mile from your house, a two foot gully washer blocks the road. Stymied yet again, a stranger standing beside his low down convertible assures us *There's a way around this.* Laughing tears, I think ... *If only.*

LAST ENCOUNTER

Watering the rose bushes,
I spot a momma cottontail
and three newborns nestled
in the decaying mulch.

I back away, and
during the night
they disappear.

A few days later,
one of the babies wanders
onto the front steps
and sits there stone still
staring at me.

I pluck a blade of grass
and ease it toward the tip
of her unflinching nose
till she finally scampers
behind the lilac bush,
and I think *Good enough.*

ANTICIPATION
~ October 9th, 2017

I finish ahead
of our first storm

    trimming the yard
    repainting the deck.

Part of me looks forward
to the soft flakes

    the escape from
    summer dog days,

and yet another part dreads
sloshing ankle deep

    brooming-off branches bent
    flat to the ground.

But *No matter*
I say to myself

    Just an old man wondering
    what's next.

Made in the USA
Middletown, DE
19 May 2019